CELTS
◁ MYTHS AND LEGENDS ▷

Translated by Abigail Frost
Illustrations by Marcel Laverdet
Original version by Bernard Briais
Edited by Gilles Ragache

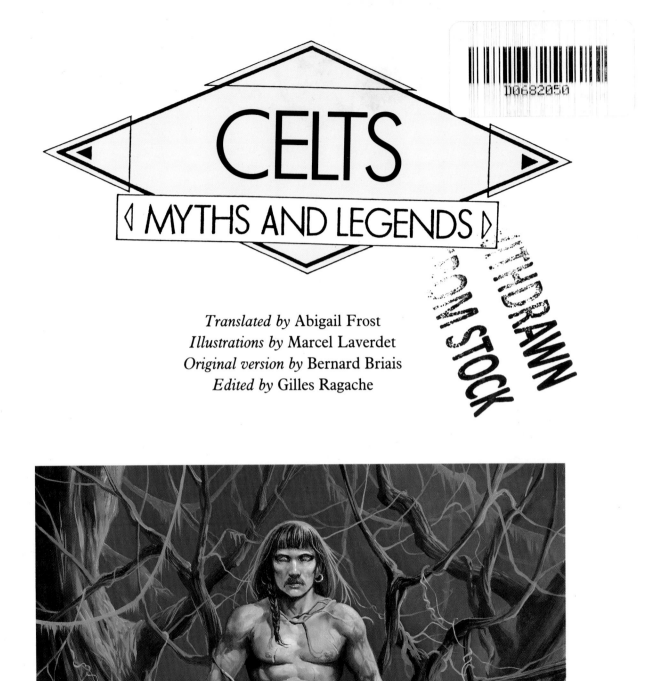

CHERRYTREE BOOKS

A Cherrytree Book

Adapted by A S Publishing
from *Les Gaulois*
published by Hachette

First published 1991
by Cherrytree Press Ltd
a subsidiary of
The Chivers Company Ltd
Windsor Bridge Road
Bath, Avon BA2 3AX

Reprinted 1993, 1996

British Library Cataloguing in Publication Data
Celts.
    1. Celtic myths   2. Celtic legends
    1. Frost, Abigail   II. Series   III. Gaulois. *English*
293.13

ISBN 0-7451-5121-3

Printed in Hong Kong by Colorcraft Ltd

CONTENTS

▷ THE KEEPER OF MEMORIES ◁

Most of the village people were gathered round a huge fire. They sat still on the ground, listening attentively to their bard, who stood on a log. He spoke slowly, and his deep voice seemed far older than he was.

'Many, many moons ago …' he began. He looked up at the starry sky for a moment, then started to speak again. 'In that long-ago time, the Bituriges, a warrior tribe, called themselves the "kings of the world". Their ruler was Ambigat. One spring, he called his people together:

"My people!" he said. "Our lands are blessed by the gods. Our fields give rich crops, and under the earth we have iron, most powerful of metals. But our riches will not last for ever. The day will soon come when there will be more of us than the land can support. But all around us is a world of even greater riches. Remember last summer, when merchants came from the East, with delicious figs and grapes, and wine like the nectar of the gods? Who would not like to visit the wonderful country those came from? We do not have roots on our feet – from earliest times, we Celts have been wandering the world, and now it may be time to set off again."

'Hardly had the chief stopped speaking, when his two nephews rose: "Your words are wise," they said. "Tomorrow, we shall leave to find new lands. Which men are brave enough to follow us? The gods will guide us!"

'Nobody slept that night: all was bustle as the two groups of young warriors, their wives and their children gathered up their possessions and their livestock ready for their journey.

'One group, led by Bellovesus, went South, into the north of Italy – the lands the Romans call "Cisalpine Gaul". The other, under Sigovessus, went North, into the centre of Europe. And so it was that our people spread throughout the world.'

The bard fell silent, and the people quietly stood up and went back to their homes. They came each night to listen to the bard's stories of the tribe's past; tales of wars and epic journeys, of great warriors and brave queens.

None of these tales was written down: the bards would have scorned writing if they knew about it. 'What would happen to memory if it was never used?' they would probably have said. The bards remembered the whole history of the Celtic people, and made sure their sons knew it by heart, too, so that the tradition was carried on. And so the Celts kept centuries of history alive in stories.

The bards' traditions outlived all trace of the world that had produced them. Their tales continued when the Celtic gods were forgotten, and so were the names and family trees of the rulers who had once seemed so important. But in the end, even the bards were silenced, and their names forgotten too.

'Tomorrow, we shall leave to find new lands. The gods will guide us wherever we go!' The Celts were fearless people, always ready for adventure.

▷ THE RAGE OF TARANIS ◁

The two men had been climbing for many hours. They had passed the tree-line and were walking up towards the clouds. They thought how silent it was up there. No humans or animals ever came up this high, yet they could somehow sense the presence of another being. They felt for their swords, just in case. Now they began to regret having taken up a stupid dare at the end of a drunken feast: to climb to the very top of the sacred mountain. They must have been mad!

Taranis, the great god of the skies, looked down at the nervous pair. He frowned, and stroked his beard thoughtfully. How dare these insolent men enter a god's territory!

The men paused. The world below appeared so small and far away. They seemed to be in another universe. The wind was rising and the sky grew dark. Perhaps they should turn back while there was still time. But it was not far to the top, and giving up would mean disgrace. They walked on.

Now Taranis was angry. He seized a lightning-bolt and aimed it carefully at Earth. The sky was torn apart by a jagged streak of blinding fire. At the same time, there was a long, loud thunderclap; the rumble of the god's chariot-wheels as he charged ahead at the men. Nobody invades Taranis's domain and gets away with it!

The men huddled together in terror, a feeling neither had really known before. They would much rather be on the battlefield, facing mortal enemies with weapons they understood. They threw down their swords to ask for a truce – but would the god accept their surrender? They were certain that the sky was about to fall on their heads.

In desperation, they called the god of their tribe: Teutates. He protected them from war, famine and plague; but could he help them against another god? At home, Taranis's anger was appeased with human sacrifices. Were the two climbers fated to be sacrificed too, burnt alive by lightning?

The rocks around them seemed to take on strange and sinister shapes. They thought of old stories they had heard as children, and shivered. But Taranis, at last, grew tired of threatening the two men. They had learnt their lesson, and besides, he had almost used up all his lightning-bolts. He turned his chariot round and rode away.

The men could still hear the thunder, but it grew fainter and more distant all the time. They hurried down towards the safety of the forests. It would be a long time before they or anyone else dared climb the sacred mountain. They would treat it, and the god who lived on it, with more respect in future.

Taranis's lightning-bolt tore the sky apart.

MISTLETOE

Six nights had passed after the new moon, and a slender crescent lit the sky. A light blanket of snow covered the ground. The men and women of the village had wrapped themselves carefully against the cold, in thick, hooded cloaks of wool dyed in many colours. However bad the weather, they could not miss the ceremony to be held that night. Everyone, old or young, from the noblest warrior to the poorest herdsman, walked behind the white-robed druid towards the sacred forest. With them they brought two white oxen, yoked for the first time, which walked slowly and with an air of resignation.

The path became steeper as they neared the forest's edge. The druid stopped for a moment to let his followers regroup; then he led them into the dark, mysterious world of the forest – a world without sky, its only horizon numberless tree-trunks. As the wind rose, the branches seemed to speak in answer to the druid's chant. Could the old man speak the language of the trees?

The path itself faded under the people's feet, and with it all trace of their own familiar world. Now they were far from their homes, their herds and their fields. But they trusted the druid who led them. At last he stopped in a clearing, and all stopped still beside him.

'The tree!' he cried, pointing at a huge, old oak tree, whose bare branches were twisted into strange and frightening shapes.

'The tree!' echoed the people. This was the moment they had come for.

High in the twisted branches was a ball of bright green leaves. As he did every year, the druid had led his people unerringly to the one tree the gods had chosen to bless; the tree where the strange plant grew, which did not have roots in the ground, and which bore green leaves when all the other plants were bare. We call this plant 'mistletoe' today. For the Celts, mistletoe seemed to come from another world, that of the gods and of the dead. Its green leaves growing from the tree's bare branches symbolised life coming out of death.

The people formed a circle round the sacred tree. The druid, old and shaky though he was, began to climb the tree. Once he had got a firm footing on the lowest branch, the climb was easy. He carried with him a sickle of gold – that wonderful metal which looks like the sun itself and which never tarnishes. Chanting strange words, he reached the top of the tree, and cut down the mistletoe with one practised blow. As he did so, on the ground below the two white oxen were sacrificed to the gods.

The snow was falling faster as the villagers set off for home. All would be well for another year, because they were bringing back the magic plant from the kingdom of the dead.

The druid cut down the mistletoe with one practised slash.

9

To the Romans, it seemed as if the trees themselves were fighting on the Celts' side!

THE FOREST GODS DO BATTLE

Huge forests covered much of Europe in Celtic times. The greatest of them all took sixty days' march to cross. The forest was sacred to the Celts, and it was a friend to them, especially in times of war. A small Celtic band could hold out against a Roman army in the forest. And sometimes, the forest gods could help the Celts to victory . . .

The Roman consul Postumius Lucius led 25,000 men against the Boii, a Celtic tribe who lived in northern Italy. His legions marched smartly together; they were the best-disciplined soldiers in the world. But when they reached the forest of Litena, they all shivered like the rawest of recruits. The forest, with its strange shadows and thick undergrowth, was a terrible enemy to the Roman army, trained to fight in good light and plenty of space.

The Boii knew what the Romans feared and set a trap for them. All along the woodland paths, they carefully cut the tree trunks so that they remained upright – but the slightest touch would bring them falling down. Then they hid in the undergrowth.

As Postumius's men marched into the forest's depths, the hidden Boii pushed over the trees nearest to them. As each tree fell, it knocked over its neighbour, which knocked over another, and so on, until half the forest had fallen into the Romans' path. It was as if the trees were fighting on the Boii's side!

Many Roman soldiers died or were terribly injured under the falling trees. Those who survived the trees faced a worse terror – the fierce Celtic warriors defending their land. The Boii were not afraid to die. They scorned even to wear armour, fighting naked except for their helmets, rich gold bracelets and torques (metal necklaces).

Postumius fought bravely, though many of his men were paralysed with terror. But the Boii caught him in the end and cut off his head. They carried it home in triumph, and covered his skull with gold. They used it, so the Romans chroniclers said, as a vessel from which to pour sacred wine in their temple.

They took home other things as well: all the Romans' weapons, armour and jewellery. These they piled up in a sacred place as a lasting thanks to the gods for their victory. The treasure was quite safe, even unguarded. Any man who stole even part of it knew he would be cursed by the gods forever.

THE GROVE OF HORROR

The Roman poet Lucan, who lived in the first century AD, wrote a description of a sacred Celtic grove: a cold, dark and shady place, whose tangled boughs kept all the sunlight out. Pan, Silvanus and the Nymphs (the Roman gods and spirits of the woods) did not live there; but other gods were worshipped there with horrific rites. Altars were heaped with hideous sacrifices, and every tree was sprinkled with human blood.

THE WISDOM OF THE CROWS

Birds fascinated the Celts; they seemed to understand the will of the gods. They could travel up in the air, nearer the gods than people could go; so naturally, they could bring messages from them. Sometimes the Celts would ask the birds – especially crows – to settle a dispute.

It would happen like this. Perhaps two neighbours were quarrelling about who had the right to a swarm of bees – and the honey they would provide. The druid would have to decide, but he must be sure that everyone would regard his decision as fair. The best thing to do was to leave it to the gods, who would send their decision through the druid's tame crows.

The druid took his crows to the tree where the bees were gathered, and put two cakes down, one on one neighbour's side of the tree, one on the other's. Then he let the crows out of their cage. Their wings had been clipped so that they could not fly away.

All the village watched as the crows turned towards the cakes. One they ate hungrily, the other they scattered to the wind with their wings. The man whose cake was broken up owned the swarm of bees. Everyone was quite satisfied with this decision – after all, it was a message from the gods.

THE CROWS' TOWN

A strange procession was crossing the countryside of Gaul; thousands of young men were travelling with their women and with all their belongings on ox-carts. They were led by two handsome young princes on horseback and a pair of wise old druids. They had set out at the height of spring to find a new home, and would not stop until the druids told them the place was right.

At last they came to a place where two rivers met, in a wide and fertile valley. It seemed a good spot in which to settle. The princes called their followers to a halt, and while they looked around, everyone else set up camp, glad of the chance of a rest.

Soon a meal had been cooked and eaten, and everyone was dropping off to sleep – except the druids. They stayed awake to find out what the gods thought. Next morning they told the princes what they had learnt. A hill to the west was the favoured site. It had a good view of the surrounding country, so it would be easy to defend. The land above the marshy ground near the river was dry and firm.

But first the princes had to make sure that the gods approved. One of them took up a plough and started to draw it along the edge of the hill. When he became tired, his brother took over. The druids watched for signs of the gods' will.

And then the sign came. Thousands of crows suddenly flew over the horizon and started to follow the plough. The princes continued ploughing until they had gone almost completely round the hill. Then the crows, as if at a signal, landed in the furrow all together just as the circuit was completed. This was the sign from the gods. The princes decided to call their town Lugdunum – 'the crows' hill'. Today it is still a thriving French town, called Lyons.

Thousands of crows flew after the plough.

THE BOUNTY OF CERNUNNOS

Deep in the forest a strange stag had been seen. It was far bigger and had finer, more branching antlers than the other animals which the hunters knew well. People noticed the white crescent of hairs on its forehead, and knew who it was: 'The lord of the forest!'

This stag did not fear the hunters. It watched them with an air of amusement, knowing that they were just the latest in a long line of humans. The stag was older than all of them, and would outlive them all. And it could take more than one shape . . .

As the hunters watched, the stag turned quickly and ran off into the forest. The men tried to follow its track, but soon got lost. They found themselves at the foot of a rocky hill.

Normally they would have turned back, but something made them press on, up towards a cavern in the rocks.

Deep in the cavern sat Cernunnos, an old, mysterious god. He could remember the time when humans could barely talk, and had to make their tools and weapons from stones, because they had not yet learnt how to forge bright, beautiful metals. In those days, they had lived in his cave, and painted his picture on the walls. Now they lived far away, in houses they built themselves, but they still respected him, if they knew what was good for them.

The men entered the cavern, despite its dark and frightening atmosphere. They turned a corner and saw the god.

14

He sat cross-legged, and was dressed like the warriors of their tribe, in trousers and cloak, with golden jewellery: a belt, a bracelet and a magnificent torque. He would have been an impressive sight for his jewellery alone, but there was much more. He had the many-branching antlers of a fine stag – in fact, of the finest of all, the 'lord of the forest'. And his feet were hoofs.

This was Cernunnos, the shape-changer, the horned god who brought prosperity. The men bent their heads in respect. The god took a sack from the rocks beside him, and poured out its contents: gold coins, to reward the human creatures who had come to worship him.

The cave grew darker. The men could no longer see the god. They looked from one to the other, wondering if this could be true. Was it a dream? Maybe it was – but the sack of gold was real enough. The god of riches, lord of the forest, had given a wonderful gift to his people.

Cernunnos emptied a sack of gold coins to reward his worshippers.

EPONA THE HORSEWOMAN

The Celts admired horses, which were among a chief's most valued possessions. When the Gaulish chief Vercingetorix was besieged by the Romans, he sent his horses away into the country in case they were hurt. Celtic farmers bred horses for both riding and drawing chariots and other vehicles. They made fine leather and metal bridles for their horses. Images of horses decorate much fine Celtic metalwork. And over much of the Roman empire are found images of a horse-goddess. Sometimes she is shown riding side-saddle, sometimes accompanied by a pair of mares, or a mare and foal. This is Epona, a goddess of fertility, who had a special relationship with all who bred, rode or cared for horses. The Roman cavalry – many of whom were Gauls originally – took her for their own protector.

Epona helped those who tamed and trained horses too. In some parts of the Celtic world, herds of horses lived free in the forests, just as the New Forest ponies do today. They would fend for themselves – but the Celts would catch the best of their foals every year to break in for riding, pulling carts or for breeding.

Breaking in a foal took patience. The animal would be frightened at first, and for a long time unwilling to let its captors come too near. The trainer had to gain its confidence with food and reassuring noises long before he could put a bridle on it or teach it to accept a rider. The idea of a friendly, protective goddess working on his side must often have given a horse-trainer confidence when working with a difficult animal.

A well-trained horse was of immense value in a society like the Celts'. A horse that would not panic when ridden in battle, or that would pull a heavy load without complaint for miles; these were worth their weight in gold. A good horse-breeder would know which mare and stallion to bring together to breed a foal that would grow up into a fast horse, a patient horse, or an extra strong horse. Knowledge of this kind demanded a special goddess.

Epona helps to capture a wild foal.

▷ THE SERPENTS' EGG ◁

The druid made the sacrifice to the gods, then mounted his horse and rode off down the road. He had told nobody where he was going. The curious villagers talked of little else. Might he be heading to the great meeting of the druids in the forests of Gaul? But it was the wrong time of year. Was he heading for the mysterious island of Anglesey?

Many nights passed, and at last the druid arrived home. Everyone crowded round him to hear why he had gone away, and where. Silencing their questions with a gesture of his hand, the druid told his story:

'I have been travelling in deserted lands in search of a wonderful thing, which will help us all. I did not tell you where I was going, because I was forbidden to do so.

'It was a long journey, and difficult sometimes. I rode mainly by night, so that I could find my way by the stars. I was heading north. Once I crossed a battlefield, where two neighbouring tribes were fighting fiercely over some land. But they let me pass without question. As a druid, I can go wherever I like in perfect safety.

'I passed through many other lands, and met all sorts of people. Some were friendly, others treated me coldly; but none tried to harm me or stop my quest. At last, I came to a region where no one lived. I rode on until I reached the edge of a forest. I had almost reached my journey's end.

'I built myself a shelter of branches, and settled down to wait for the new moon. Just as it rose, I mounted my horse and entered the dark wood. It was difficult getting through the tangled branches; no man had ever been there before me. It was a hot night, and everything was very still. I did not hear so much as a bird's wing flutter.

'The sun's first rays broke through the branches. It was time to dismount. Now I could hear something. It was a faint hissing.

'I followed the noise and found myself in a clearing. The sight before me rooted me to the spot. A great mass of vipers writhed on the ground, thousands of them coiled together. The sunlight gleamed on their sleek skin. Now their hissing was far from faint. They were hissing at me, angry at being disturbed.

'Their venom spurted into the middle of the clearing, drying up quickly in the hot sun. As they coiled and writhed, their bodies rolled it into a ball, like a huge egg. It was white, with a thin, leathery skin. I knew it was a thing of monstrous magical power.

'The snakes hissed harder and harder, and gradually the egg rose up, floating on their poisoned breath.

'This was my chance. I tore off a piece of my

cloak, and caught the egg in it. Now the snakes were really angry. Quickly I mounted my horse and galloped off. They rose up out of their nest, and slithered furiously after me, hissing and spitting.

'I called for help to the god of our tribe; and almost as I spoke the undergrowth seemed less thick. There was fresh green grass under the horse's hooves. Now I could keep ahead of the dreadful serpents. At last we came to a river which the snakes could not cross. I thanked the god as we crossed it, and rode on home, glad to have the magic egg to use to help my people.'

The druid has captured the egg, but can he escape the vipers?

TALL TALE

The Roman author Pliny the Elder, who wrote about curious animals from faraway lands, met someone who had 'seen the druid's magical serpents' egg'. But from his description, it was more likely to be the egg-case of a sea-creature such as a whelk. Pliny would not have recognized such a thing, because whelks do not live in the Mediterranean Sea, although their eggs are a familiar sight on Atlantic beaches.

19

THE CHAINS OF ELOQUENCE

The Greek poet Lucian who lived in the second century AD travelled all over Europe noticing examples of the power of words. As a young man, he had been apprenticed first to a sculptor, then to a lawyer, but he hated both professions; he thought that to be a poet was the highest calling there was and that words were magic. The Gauls (Celts who lived in present-day France) agreed with him.

Stopping at a Gaulish town, Lucian noticed a strangely carved stone. It showed an old man, dressed like the Greek hero Heracles, in a lion-skin. It was puzzling enough that a feeble old man should wear the clothes of a strongman, but even stranger that he was leading a crowd of people by fine chains attached to his tongue.

Lucian asked a Greek-speaking Gaul what the carving meant. 'That is our god Ogmios,' he said. 'He is stronger than your Heracles, although he is very old, because he is god of eloquence. Through the power of his tongue, his beautiful words, he can lead people wherever he chooses; and he does not have to force them to follow him. They come willingly, and praise him all the time. His words are like beautifully wrought chains of fine gold and amber. A man who has such chains at his disposal is more powerful than the strongest man on earth. Though he is physically weak himself, he can make strong men fight for the cause he supports, and lead them to the dark caves of death if need be.'

Delighted by this story, Lucian wrote it down in one of his poems.

Ogmios captured human minds, with words like chains of gold.

The young fisherman always made certain to keep close to the shore. The open sea was much too dangerous for his fragile little boat. But one hot day, lulled by the boat's gentle rocking as the water was fanned by a faint breeze, he dozed off. He woke, confused and frightened, to deep black night, and a howling storm.

How could he be so stupid? Where was he? He could not see the shore he knew so well. The night was so cloudy he could not even see the stars. But he had no time to dwell on these worries. It took all his efforts to keep his boat afloat as the waves tossed it about. He was absolutely alone. The Celts did not have a sea-god, so there was nobody he could call on for help.

At last the wind began to drop, and he relaxed a little. He could hear the cries of sea-gulls. The birds gave him new hope. Gulls never fly very far from land. He gazed into the darkness, but he could not see far enough. Then his boat hit a rock. He must have come upon an island.

Exhausted, but glad to be alive, he pulled his boat up on to the shore. It was damaged, but he thought he could mend it later. He looked around to see what kind of place he had landed on. Were there people there? Far away, he noticed a glow like that of a camp fire. Thinking of food, dry clothes and helping hands, he set off in that direction.

Suddenly he stopped in astonishment. Down below were a group of women dancing wildly round a fire, in front of a wooden temple with a thatched roof. As they danced they made strange, chilling cries. The fisherman knew where he was, now.

'This is the forbidden island! These are its priestesses!'

There were many terrible tales about the

The priestesses danced and sang strange chants.

island. But there was no immediate way to escape. The young man hid in the undergrowth and watched the scene below.

The women stopped dancing. They stood quite still, facing east. As the sun's first rays lit the horizon, a long cry broke the silence. The women turned towards the temple as if to enter it, but instead, they took ladders and climbed up on to the roof. They began to tear down the thatch and throw it on to the fire.

By noon, the temple was open to the skies, and the fire burning brightly. Now the women gathered up branches and straw, and began to make a new roof. They started by arranging the branches into a frame, and then they set to work on the thatch. They laid bundles of straw next to each other and tied them together.

The fisherman admired their skill and speed, but was frightened by their merciless cruelty. If one of them dropped her load of straw on the ground, the others fell upon her and killed her for her sacrilege.

By the time the sun began to set, the temple had a brand-new roof. Now the women went inside. Perhaps they had a ceremony to perform. The fisherman saw his chance to escape. Down on the beach, he found his boat, and managed to fill up the hole with some of his clothes. Quickly he set sail across the now-calm waters. He would take care to stay within sight of land from now on. What might they have done to him if they had caught him prying?

THE MARRIAGE OF GYPTIS

Nanus, king of the Segobriges, was holding a great feast at his home by the Mediterranean Sea. On the beach his servants had set up a huge table covered with food. There were not enough seats for all his guests, so some had spread skins or straw on the ground to sit on. Everyone was laughing, talking or singing, and the noise drowned the sound of the waves.

In a nearby house waited Gyptis, the king's eldest daughter. This was an important day for her. Her father had decreed that she was old enough to choose a husband; soon she would be summoned to select one of her many suitors. But first the men must have their feast.

Gyptis was dressed in her best, with her finest jewellery, and she had made her hair shine brightly with a secret mixture of egg-yolk and ashes. Impatiently, she tried on a fine gold

coronet at different angles.

The feast was in full swing. Over a huge fire, wild boar were roasting on spits. As each guest finished his portion of meat, he threw the bones down for the dogs to eat. The food was so good that nobody noticed two strangers walking towards them. The guests went on eating, until suddenly a man addressed the king in Greek: 'Hail, great king of the Segobriges!'

Everyone stopped talking. The king (who understood Greek well) asked the speaker who he was. 'I am Protis and this is my brother Simon. We have sailed here from the shores of the Aegean Sea, and we want to stay here. Great king, will you let us have a portion of your land?'

Nanus invited the Greeks to join the feast. The curious Celts crowded round them and asked about their homeland. The king translated the questions and answers, and soon everyone was joining in.

Gyptis, watching from her room, could not understand why the feast was taking so long. She decided to break the rules and go down to the beach. As she approached the men, she felt nervous. Everyone seemed to be watching her. But when her father greeted her warmly, she felt better.

The king was proud of his brave and beautiful daughter. He handed her a goblet of water. She was to offer it to the man she chose.

Gyptis carefully looked at the guests. Her heart beat faster when she saw the handsome young Greek, Protis. Blushing a little, she offered him the goblet. He took it from her.

The king hugged the two young people. He was glad Gyptis had chosen well; he had long admired the Greeks. As a wedding gift, he gave his new son-in-law a piece of land beside the sea.

Here, Protis and his Greek followers built a city, which they called Massilia. Today, it is called Marseilles, and it is an important port in southern France.

The beautiful Gyptis went down to the beach to meet her suitors.

25

▷ A STRANGE CUSTOMER ◁

The red-faced smith was like a friendly giant. He was the biggest and strongest man in the village, and was always cheerful. When he laughed, his eyes danced in the fire-light. He seemed to fear nothing.

All the villagers liked and respected him. Often, the ringing of his hammer woke them in the morning. But there was something strange about him too. People said he had a magic hammer, which could make iron sing. His forge was a secret sanctuary, where, with the help of the fire, he made the hard metal obey his will. With his hammer he made swords for the warriors, axes for the woodsmen and ploughs for the farmers.

He had learned the secrets of metal-working from his father. The craft had been passed down in their family over many years. He believed that a god, Ucuetis, had first taught his ancestors to shape red-hot iron on an anvil. The skill was jealously guarded; it was iron, and the ability to make weapons from it, which had helped the Celts in battles against other peoples whose weapons were of softer metal.

The forge was always hot, and sometimes, if he was busy, the smith would work on into the cool of the evening. Once, he was clearing up after a long day. It was quite dark and silent outside. Suddenly, the calm was broken by three loud knocks on the door.

At the door stood a tall, strong man, carrying an axe. The smith noticed that its edge was damaged. The man held it out and asked the smith to mend it.

It was late, and the smith had already damped down his fire for the night. But he felt, somehow, that he should not keep this stranger waiting. Quickly he put charcoal on the dying fire, and pumped away at a bellows, until it was glowing hot again. Then he put the axe-head into the hottest part of the fire, and again blew more air into it with the bellows. After a long time, the heavy iron axe-head was red-hot and ready to work. He gripped it in a pair of tongs (he had made them himself, when he was a boy working with his father) and carried it over to the anvil.

As he hit the axe with his heavy hammer, the crack along its edge closed up. Under the pressure, the metal bonded back together, until it was as good as new. But it had taken a long time. Dawn was breaking as the stranger took his axe away.

Why had the smith worked all night to mend a stranger's axe? Perhaps he thought it was better to be safe than sorry. He knew that in the forests lived a harsh and cruel god, called Esus. Men were sacrificed to him, left hanging from trees; and he would cut the trees down with his terrible axe.

The smith was not a talkative man, and when people asked why he had been working all night, he simply said that he had been doing a job for a special customer.

The smith hammered the red-hot axe-head until it was as good as new.

THE GEESE THAT SAVED THE CITY

The Celtic chief gazed at the jagged Apennine mountains on the horizon. Behind him, three hundred thousand armed men watched in silence. He had promised fame and glory to those brave enough to cross the range with him and attack Rome itself.

The longest day of summer was approaching and the moon would soon be full. The druids said this was the most favourable time to attack. On the other side of a small river the Roman army waited, determined to stop the advance of the 'barbarian hordes'. But when the Celtic forces raised their war-cry, the Romans fled! To the Celts, this was yet another proof of the magic power of words.

So far, things had gone well. When the chief and his men reached Rome they were astonished to find the gates wide open. All was still within the city walls. The Celts nervously explored the deserted streets of the world's greatest city. Was this a trick?

They turned a corner and found another great surprise. There sat a dozen grand old men in ivory chairs, quite still and silent. These were the city's chief magistrates. The Celts stared at them. Were they men or statues? Then one bold warrior pulled a 'statue's' beard – and it hit him hard with its rod of office.

Suddenly the Celts were angry. They rampaged through the city, killing all who resisted, and tearing down temples and houses alike.

But one part of the city they could not take: the great Capitoline Hill, which was the seat of the government of Rome. The Romans had decided to defend it to the death. No matter how hard the Celts fought, the Romans always drove them down again.

One dark night, the Celts made a surprise attack. They decided to climb the hill in the silence of the night. All went well as they inched their way up the rocky path and approached the buildings at the summit. There were no sentries, it seemed, not even a guard dog to protect the heart of Rome.

But suddenly the most terrible noise broke out, something between the hissing of a snake, the barking of a dog and the laughter of a madman, with a heavy beating sound mixed in. Terrified, the Celtic warriors stopped, and one or two fell back. Those who tumbled took others down with them. What horrible monster could they have disturbed?

The Romans awoke. They knew what had saved the Capitol. It was the sacred geese that lived in the temple of the goddess Juno, hissing, cackling and beating their wings.

But for the watchful geese, the Celts would have captured the temple.

31

THE HAMMER OF SUCELLUS

The old chief slept, stretched out in his chariot. His face was as pale and still as that of a marble statue. There seemed no sign now of the agony he had suffered when a spear transfixed his body. His beautiful shield hid the wound from view. At his right side was his favourite sword, with its hilt of finely-wrought bronze set with coral. He had been so proud of it!

His house was filled with weeping. His eldest daughter seemed inconsolable, though many tried to comfort her, telling her how bravely her father had died. But, as six of his warriors led the chariot out of the house, she clenched her fists tight to stop herself crying.

The funeral procession crossed the village slowly. When it reached the boundary ditch, the first of many ceremonies took place. The village smith took the chief's sword, and heated it in a fire he had ready. When the blade was

Sucellus, with his mighty hammer, could kill or restore life.

red-hot, he bent it back on itself with his hammer. Then he punched a hole in the metal centre of the chief's magnificent shield. The chief was going to a land of peace, and his weapons must be broken accordingly.

At the tomb, the chief's son placed a small statue of a horse beside his father's body, to lead the old man to the next world. Other rich grave-goods followed; then the grave was filled in and given a roof of stone. The chief's friends talked about him. One remembered how, only a few days before, he had given him some money, to be repaid in the next world. Others agreed that the chief was a generous man. Meanwhile, his spirit was going on its journey.

At the gates of the next world, Sucellus waited to welcome the chief. He was the god of death, and the god of healing. He was dressed like a Celtic chief himself, in a cloak, tunic and trousers, and he carried a heavy hammer. A blow from one side of its head would kill; but a blow from the other would bring the dead back to life, in the world of the spirits.

Sucellus silently handed the chief a pottery cup; once he had drunk the water in it, the chief would be immortal. His death had been just an interruption in a long, long life.

Meanwhile, back on Earth, the bards of the chief's tribe were declaiming long poems about his exploits, while ordinary people shovelled soil over his grave, until a huge, circular mound marked the spot.

As the years passed, the grass would grow over the mound, and far off in the future, people would wonder what was under it. Was it the entrance to fairyland, perhaps? Legends grew up about a giant in golden armour who lived beneath the mound. Nobody realised how close that was to the truth.

THE LADY OF VIX

In the Burgundy region of France is the site of the Celtic town of Vix. In 1953, archaeologists discovered a tomb there, in a timber-lined shaft under a mound of stones. It was the tomb of a young woman, who must have died around 500 BC. She wore a gold coronet decorated with two winged horses, and golden bracelets, necklaces and other jewellery.

She was buried sitting in a four-wheeled chariot which was designed to be pulled by people, not horses. With her was a huge vase, big enough to hold 1,200 litres. It seems not to have been made in France, but imported from Greece.

Nobody knows who the buried woman was. Perhaps she was a princess, or a priestess, or a warrior queen like the much later Boudicca. But her magnificent burial shows that women had high status among the Celts.

▷ SEQUANA ◁

A crowd was gathering where the great river sprang up out of the ground. Some had travelled many miles to ask the help of Sequana, the goddess who ruled the spring. The Celts believed that she could cure the illnesses they most feared, and help them in all their troubles.

Among the pilgrims was a woman who seemed unable to have a child. Her husband was afraid he would never have a son to take over his workshop when he himself grew too old to work. Would the couple starve in their old age? Beside her was a man from her village. His eyesight was growing worse, year after year; he was afraid that soon he would be blind. So the two had travelled together to ask kind Sequana to help.

They had walked all the way, leaning on staffs and wrapped up well in their best cloaks. The journey had taken several weeks, and they had slept at night under the stars, listening carefully for the sounds of wild beasts.

As they climbed higher, they noticed dozens of makeshift stalls by the road. The stallholders shouted to attract their attention. They were selling offerings to the goddess. The offerings, carved in wood or cast in metal, to suit all pockets, were in the shape of small figures, or of parts of the body. The woman who wanted to have a child bought a wooden figure, and scratched her name on the back. The man who feared blindness bought a bronze plaque with a pair of eyes on it. The goddess would understand.

Now the two pilgrims looked around. They had never seen so many people in one place before. It was the season for visits to the shrine, the one time of the year when the weather was favourable for travelling, and there was not too much to be done on the farms. And all the people had some trouble or other. Some were lame, others blind; some had terrible diseases which disfigured them. Some were too ill to walk, and had been carried on wooden stretchers by their relatives. Others looked strong and well, but terribly sad.

The new arrivals shivered. Here were so many worse off than they were! Perhaps they should not bother the goddess. She must be very busy. But having come all this way, they decided to continue. They walked down some steps and found themselves at a pool, dug from the rock. Here they could drink the healing waters, and leave their offerings.

Three times the pilgrims walked round the temple and prayed to the goddess. Then they went to the pool. It was divided into sections for men and women, so they had to split up. The woman jumped up to her neck in the cold, clear water; the man was content to lie down at its edge and bathe his eyes.

Once they had finished the healing ritual, they immediately began to feel better. They remembered tales of people who had been cured almost at once after drinking the water. On the way out, the man spoke to a priest about his eyes. The priest gave him a box of paste; if he mixed a little of it every night with the sacred water, it would make an ointment for his eyes.

The woman felt better and more relaxed than she had for years. Perhaps next year she would have a baby. The pair bought a vase from one of the stallholders, and filled it with the sacred water. It would be heavy to carry home – but think how many family illnesses it might cure!

The sick and hopeful left offerings at the shrine of the healing river-goddess.

The Celts have left us images of their gods, and of other things that they thought important, in some of their works of art. Among these are images of unreal animals so strange that nobody can now understand what meaning they had for the Celts. They must have been made-up creatures from long lost myths.

Stone carvings have been found which show Tarvostrigaranus, a bull with three cranes perched on its back. There are also carvings and metal figures of three-headed gods, three-horned animals and three goddesses trans-formed into birds. Three has been thought of as a magic number in many cultures.

Another strange creature which the Celts often depicted is a snake with a ram's head.

This monster seems to exist only in Celtic art, never in other peoples' stories or art. Some scholars think the Celts imagined it as a creature of the underworld. Snakes may well have appeared to them as supernatural because they shed their old skins each year. The ram-horned snake often appears in art with other gods or goddesses, especially the horned god of the forests, Cernunnos.

We know from much later legends that the Celts believed their gods were shape-changers – they could go from human shape to animal in a twinkling. In later tales, written down in Christian times, shape-changing is often a talent of magicians. Perhaps some of the beasts in Celtic art are gods in animal shape.

A MAGIC CAULDRON?

Many strange beasts are to be seen on the Gundestrup Bowl, a large silver cauldron found in Denmark in 1880, and a great treasure of early art. Scenes from mythology are beautifully worked on both its inside and outside. Although the Celts did not live in Denmark, scholars think that it may be Celtic work, and the pictures on it certainly seem to show Celtic gods. Perhaps Viking invaders plundered it from Britain.

Cauldrons, being containers of water, had a double significance in Celtic religion. They brought both life and death. Bathing in water from a sacred cauldron could restore lost youth and health. But such cauldrons may also have been used to catch the blood of sacrificial victims. The Gundestrup Bowl itself shows a god holding a man over a cauldron, and some Roman authors say that people were drowned in cauldrons of water as sacrifices.

▷ FAITHFUL EPONINA ◁

When the wicked emperor Nero killed himself, the people of Rome rejoiced. The city and the empire were in chaos. It was a good time for a rebellion. Many Celtic tribes rose up in the hope of regaining their freedom before the new emperor was crowned.

One rebel tribe, led by Sabinus, was defeated by a tribe which took the Romans' side. Sabinus managed to escape the massacre and reach his own home, where he found his loyal servant Martial.

Martial later came out of the house in tears. He said that he had been unable to prevent his master sacrificing himself by drinking a cup of poison. The chief's last wish was for his house to be set on fire. It became a huge funeral pyre for him.

Sabinus's wife Eponina threw herself to the ground in tears. For three days and nights she refused to eat; she hoped to die of grief. But, unknown to her, Sabinus was still alive, hiding in a cave. When Martial told him Eponina was close to death, he agreed that she should be told his secret.

From now on, Eponina led a double life. By day, she lived with her parents in the town, like a virtuous, grieving widow. But by night she slipped away down a secret path into the woods, to stay with her husband. She had to be careful. The Romans had spies everywhere.

For nine years nobody suspected a thing. Eponina even had two children secretly in the cave, where they stayed with their father. But finally the secret came out. Eponina left the cave one morning to find a troop of soldiers waiting for her. The whole family was arrested and taken to Rome.

Eponina's strange story was soon the talk of Rome. Many Romans secretly sympathised with this brave and loyal wife. Even the emperor Vespasian was moved by the tale, and allowed her to come and plead for mercy. But, though he listened gravely to her pleas, he still

Eponina sentenced herself to death by her defiant words to Vespasian.

would not pardon Sabinus. For 'reasons of state', he said, he must die.

Seeing there was no hope left, Eponina dried her tears. She looked the emperor in the eye and said scornfully:

'Poor Caesar! I would not exchange my destiny for yours! My life in the cave with Sabinus was a thousand times happier than your life on the throne!'

By speaking like this to the ruler of the world, Eponina had sentenced herself to death; just as she wanted. Now she and her beloved husband could go down to the next world together.

The couple were executed that very day. Their children were brought up by Roman families: one in Egypt, the other in Greece. The Roman authorities took care to keep them well away from their parents' lands, where they might have grown up to lead another rebellion.

39

▷ THE LAST DRUID IN GAUL ◁

Gaul had surrendered to the Romans. The old ways survived only in the wilderness. But one old druid in the heart of the empire held out, hiding in a forest. A few followers visited him and brought him food. But they risked their lives by doing so. The Romans, afraid that the druids might be the centre of an uprising, were dealing harshly with all who followed their ways.

Years passed. The old druid hated being in hiding, but he knew that it was essential. If he was to keep himself – and all his secret knowledge – alive, he must suffer the loneliness of his life. But one day he could stand it no longer. His followers could not persuade him to stay. Before he died, he wanted to see the new wonder of the land; the colossal statue of Mercury that the Romans had put up on top of a mountain. It was said that the sculptor, a Greek called Zenodore, had taken ten years to make it; and it had cost a true fortune – ten million silver pieces!

The druid set off, and walked for many days, taking care not to be spotted. At his first sight of the mountain – many miles away – he noticed something shining on its top. As he came nearer, he could make out its shape. Sure enough, it was the statue. His curiosity turned to anger as he looked.

How dare this strange god stand so arrogantly on top of the mountain! What an insult to the Celts and their gods! Why did great Taranis allow such a sacrilege?

As the old man struggled up the mountain, his mood changed again. He began grudgingly

The druid could not understand why the Romans worshipped a statue.

to admire the statue. First of all, its size – fifty metres high? A hundred? And yet, though it was so big, it was finely made. He knew enough about metalworking to admire the skill of its maker. But he still could not feel reverence for it. After all, it was the work of a human hand. To the druid, it did not look like a god, or suggest the presence of a god.

Under the statue was a temple, full of smaller statues. The druid asked someone about them – were they statues of great warriors, beautiful queens? No, he was told – they were gods and goddesses. The old man laughed in astonishment; these crazy Romans made their gods like ordinary men and women! The most powerful people in the world bowed down to lumps of stone!

The druid turned away, and for the first time he noticed the wonderful view from the top of the mountain. Here, in the mountains, the woods, and the great open sky – here, he thought, was where the gods were to be found. Among the trees he saw a stag run past, and thought of Cernunnos, lord of the forest. The Romans could never win, he thought. Unseen by them, the Celtic gods still ruled the land, even though Roman statues stood in the druids' holy places.

The Celts often made sculptures of heads, in wood, stone or, like this one, in bronze.

When we speak today of 'Celts', we mean people who live on the very western edges of Europe, in Ireland, Wales, Cornwall, Scotland and Brittany. The word comes from *Keltoi*, the name which Greek authors of the 5th century BC and later gave the native people of Western Europe from Spain to Czechoslovakia. The Celts also spread into Britain, Northern Italy, and parts of Asian Turkey. They were known to the Romans as the Gauls, but would have thought of themselves not as one people, but as different tribes. Celtic tribes at different times were Rome's enemies, allies and, once conquered, the soldiers, farmers and craftworkers of much of its empire.

The Celtic languages and way of life survived in the very remotest parts of the empire, and areas such as Scotland and Ireland which the Romans never conquered. When the Roman Empire fell, after five centuries of power, new conquerors swept into Britain. The Celts were forced into the wilder, hilly regions which we now call the 'Celtic fringes'; some even fled back to the Continent, and settled in the part of France called Brittany.

These later Celtic people had a rich heritage of myths, tales of heroes, fairies and giants, as well as the stories of King Arthur and his Knights of the Round Table. These stories (written down in Christian times) may be based on the tales earlier Celts told about their

Celts had settled in France by the 700s BC, in Spain and Turkey by the 200s BC, and in Britain and Ireland by the 100s BC.

gods. But we have no way of knowing. The earliest Celts had no writing of their own, and although by Roman times they were writing inscriptions on coins, gravestones and offerings to the gods, they seem to have despised writing as a way of preserving knowledge, religious rituals or stories. They preferred to rely on spoken traditions, handed down from generation to generation.

Clues from the Romans

How, then, can we know anything at all about the early Celts? There are clues in three main places. First, we can look at what Roman and Greek authors said about their Celtic neighbours. For example, Julius Caesar, the Roman general who invaded Britain in 55 BC, wrote

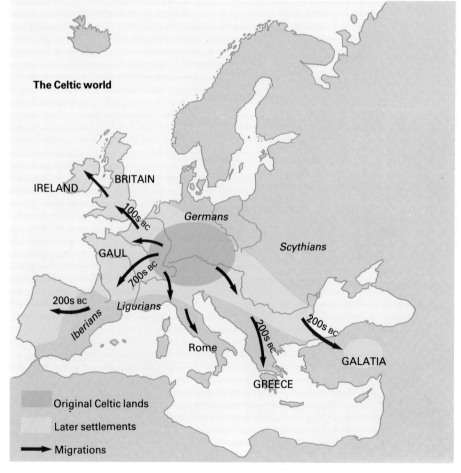

The Celtic world

IRELAND
BRITAIN
100s BC
GAUL
700s BC
Germans
Scythians
200s BC
Iberians
Ligurians
Rome
200s BC
200s BC
GREECE
GALATIA

■ Original Celtic lands
□ Later settlements
→ Migrations

This wooden carving, like those in Sequana's story (page 35), was probably made as a votive offering to a god.

an account of the invasion (and the rest of his wars against the Gauls) called *De Bello Gallico*. Caesar was as thorough an author as he was a soldier, and he put in plenty of background information about the Gauls.

But Caesar, writing from hearsay and for a Roman audience, is not a perfect guide to what the Celts thought and did. For example, he uses the names of Roman gods and goddesses instead of the Celtic ones.

Several authors tell us that the Celts made human sacrifices as part of their religion, and we have evidence of this from archaeological sites too. But when Caesar tells us that some Celtic tribes made 'huge wicker figures' which they filled with living prisoners and set on fire, it is hard not to think he is exaggerating, or telling us a garbled version, for the sake of making the Celts sound especially 'barbarous'. The 'wicker man' seems just too unlikely a method of sacrifice.

In a similar way, the Roman historian Livy tells us that the Boii used Post-

umius's severed head (see pages 10-11) as a vessel for libations – offerings of wine which the Romans poured on the ground before the statues of their gods. He probably did not know that the Celts collected the heads of their enemies and stored them in their temples. Some late Irish hero-tales mention using an enemy's skull as a drinking vessel; perhaps that was an early Celtic custom too. But Livy, not knowing exactly what the Celts did, had assumed their religion was much the same as the Romans', and fitted poor Postumius's skull into a Roman service.

Clues from archaeology

We know a little more about Celtic temples than Livy did, even though we are so much further away from them in time, because their remains have been excavated and recorded in modern times. Temples have been found with skulls carefully stored in special niches. Archaeological remains are a better source of information about Celtic religion and ritual than Caesar's and Livy's accounts, and also show us a gentler side of Celtic religion, such as the healing spring of Sequana.

Sequana's spring was the source of the River Seine, in France. During the

The Gundestrup bowl is decorated with images of Celtic gods.

1960s nearly 200 wooden offerings were found there, preserved by the damp soil. There were also remains of temple buildings and even sleeping accommodation for pilgrims.

This was just one of many sacred springs and lakes in the Celtic world. Some (like Aquae Sulis – 'Sul's waters' – in Britain, known to us as Bath) were thought to have healing powers. At others, offerings of weapons and metalwork were made; Llyn Cerrig Bach, a lake on the druids' island of Anglesey, was one such sacred place.

These Celtic traditions still survive in small ways today: 'taking the waters' at spas such as Bath used to be a common treatment for many ailments, and bottled spring water (sometimes from Celtic cult-springs, such as Buxton) is still thought to be a specially 'healthy' drink. The custom of throwing coins in a fountain or shallow pond for luck probably comes from the Celts' offerings to their gods and goddesses.

Clues from art

The Celts' own art also gives us some clues about their customs, though they are harder to interpret than the information we get from written sources or archaeological sites. The Celts were wonderful metalworkers, and decorated their work with images of gods, animals, strange monsters and half-human creatures; but we cannot always be sure

Are the creatures found in Celtic art shape-changing gods?

A bronze cockerel from France. The 'coq gaulois' is now a French national symbol.

what they mean. The Gundestrup bowl (which includes a figure of Cernunnos in its decoration) seems to be religious, but other richly-decorated objects may have been made as gifts from one chief to another. Beautifully decorated metal-work was important as a sign of wealth in Celtic society.

Some Celts, however, adopted the Roman habit of making figures of their gods, such as Taranis and Epona, and these, besides showing what the god was supposed to look like, show us indirectly who was worshipped when and where.

Both wild and domestic animals feature in the Celts' art. Sometimes animals are associated with gods (such as stag-horned Cernunnos and Epona with her mare); and metal animal figures

were made as offerings to the gods. Animals were also sacrificed to the gods; one fine stag killed in this way was buried, complete with antlers, in a tomb in France.

Horses were admired for their strength and beauty; they are often pictured on Celtic coins. The Celts trained their horses well, and enjoyed the special understanding between horse and rider. Another animal which lives and works closely with humans, the dog, is sometimes shown carved on tomb-stones, as if watching over the dead person for eternity. Besides watch-dogs, of course, the Celts had fine hounds for hunting.

Among farm-animals, cattle, poultry and pigs were all important sources of food; the cattle gave milk and leather

Wild boars were a popular subject for Celtic artists, and a favourite food for all Celts.

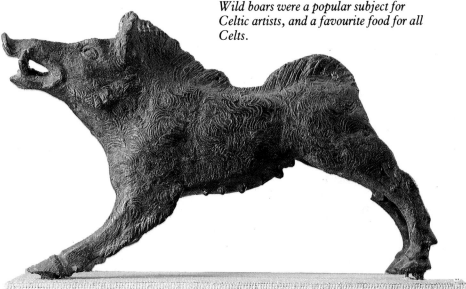

too. Both pigs and cockerels were wonderful subjects for artists, the cockerel with his crested head and magnificent tail, and the boar, like the wild ones which were also common, with tusks and a crest of bristles.

Snakes, which were a symbol of the underworld, are found in Celtic art all over Europe – except in Ireland, where there are no snakes. The legends say that St Patrick, who converted the Irish to Christianity, drove them out of the land; but in fact they never lived there.

The druids
The most famous aspect of Celtic religion must be its priests, the druids. Caesar and other Roman authors give us most of our information about them, telling us about their place among the rulers of Celtic tribes, and the secret lore they preserved in memory. Caesar (a clever politician) thought their dislike of writing things down was due to fear that if they did so, ordinary people might be able to learn their secrets and their power.

The Romans feared the druids, who seem to have been very well organized, and likely, if allowed, to stir up revolt against Roman rule. In particular, according to Caesar, they held an annual meeting in France, near modern Chartres. This suggests that the druids were able to overcome all the differences and feuds between the various tribes of Gaul, and could perhaps unite them against the Romans.

This fear persisted for a century or more after Caesar's invasion. In AD 69, after the Romans had finally conquered

The Celts borrowed the Roman habit of making statuettes of gods. This one shows Taranis.

Britain, their governor Suetonius Paulinus set out for North Wales, and the island of Anglesey, which was a druid stronghold. He met fierce resistance,

A gold torque (below left) of about 100 BC. These large necklaces were worn by Celtic chiefs as a sign of wealth and power.

A Celtic warrior's helmet (below right) of about 200 BC, finely decorated with enamel and gilding.

but finally killed all the druids. That was the end of the druids as an official power; but their poetic traditions, at least, survived in Ireland and Wales for centuries longer.

Women warriors
After Suetonius Paulinus had slaughtered the druids, he was almost immediately called away to eastern England. The revolt he feared had been started, not by the druids, but by Boudicca, Queen of the Iceni. One Roman writer describes her thus: 'Huge and terrifying to look at, with a harsh voice. She had red hair falling to her knees; she wore a huge, twisted gold torque, and a coloured tunic, and a thick mantle fastened by a brooch. She grasped a spear, striking fear into all who saw her.'

This fearsome warrior queen, whose army is said to have wiped out an entire Roman legion, is just one of many among the Celts. The woman buried at Vix (see page 33) was given the honours due to a great ruler 500 years before Boudicca; 300 years after her came the Irish tale of Queen Mehb (or Maeve), who invaded Ulster to recover a fine bull which had been taken from her herd. Lesser Celtic women could be fierce fighters too, according to Ammianus Marcellinus: 'A troop of foreigners could not beat a solitary Gaul, if he called his wife to help. A Gaulish woman is very strong ... especially when swelling her neck, gnashing her teeth, and flexing her huge arms, she begins to hit and kick, as hard as stones flying from a catapult'.

announced that scientists had found traces of blue, green and possibly red pigment on pieces of their skin, by a technique called electron probe X-ray micro-analysis.

The 'bog people' are thought to have been victims of a human sacrifice. Perhaps they were specially painted for the ceremony. Other 'bog people' have been found in Ireland, Germany and Denmark, and perhaps if their skins are tested more will be found out about the designs they wore.

The Celts under the Roman empire

During 500 years of Roman rule, the Celts adopted many Roman customs, especially where religion was concerned. The Romans had a deliberate policy of mingling local religions with their own, to help keep their subjects loyal. So, for example, Sul, the goddess of the hot springs at Bath, became known as Sul Minerva, taking on the character of the Roman goddess of wisdom. But the Romans took over some Celtic traditions too; at Bath, they turned the Celtic shrine into a magnificent bath-house. One Celtic goddess was worshipped throughout the empire – Epona, who quite naturally became a favourite of the cavalry.

In the same way, Eastern religions found their way to the Celtic people of Roman Britain: the Persian god Mithras was worshipped in temples throughout the island. And when another Eastern religion, Christianity, swept all over the empire, many Britons were converted, as we know from finding Christian symbols in late Roman-British mosaics.

About 50 years after the Romans left Britain, St Patrick began preaching Christianity in Ireland, where the Romans had never been. The church he founded was a great centre of learning, and had outposts in Northern Britain as well as Ireland. The early monks of this Celtic church wrote down the heroic tales and legends they had learnt from the spoken tradition; they also decorated religious manuscripts (such as the famous Lindisfarne Gospels) in a style which is obviously descended from the art of the pre-Roman Celts. Something of the old warrior society survived in Ireland until the early 1600s, when the ruling chieftains there finally surrendered to English rule.

Reconstruction of a Celtic barn. It is built on a timber frame, with the floor raised above the ground to keep the grain safe from damp and rats.

A metal statue of a dancer – or is she perhaps a goddess?

Ancient war-paint

Julius Caesar noted that the British Celts painted their bodies with a blue cosmetic to make themselves more terrifying in battle. The paint, called woad, came from a plant which has been used as a dye in more modern times. Scientists have now found traces of woad and other paints on the skin of two bodies preserved in a peat bog for centuries.

The bodies were discovered in Lindow Moss peat bog, in Cheshire, in 1984. One of them is now on display in the British Museum. In 1990, it was

INDEX

CONTENTS

© Archon Press Ltd 2003

Produced by
Archon Press Ltd
28 Percy Street
London W1T 2BZ

New edition first published in Great Britain in 2003 by
Franklin Watts
96 Leonard Street
London EC2A 4XD

Original edition published as
Hands on Arts and Crafts – Collage

ISBN: 0–7496–4957–7

Design: Phil Kay
Editors: Nicola Cameron and Jen Green
Drawings: Anthony Hodge
Illustrations: Ron Hayward Associates

Printed in UAE

2

Introduction

Collage, a French word meaning pasting or gluing, is a very flexible art form. It can take you beyond the limitations of paints and brushes, and introduce you to a new world of creative picture-making.

Everyone can do it

Collage can be quick and easy. It makes use of ready-made materials like photographs and paper, and is good for anyone who enjoys making images. Collage can go hand-in-hand with drawing and painting, or can be a separate activity in its own right.

New from old

Collage is cheap; it uses things people often think of as rubbish. The materials you need are all around you and can cost next to nothing. Collage is about combining familiar things in new and original ways.

About this book

This book begins with a guide to tools, techniques and materials. With the aid of projects, it guides you through simple image-making to a series of more advanced techniques.

▶ *"Scraps of polystyrene and chocolate box wrapping suggest this snow scene. I used string for the broomstick and plants, corrugated card for the house and bubble wrap for the falling snow."*

Mastering Art
COLLAGE

Anthony Hodge

Franklin Watts
London • Sydney

Tearing and Cutting

The next pages introduce some basic tools and techniques for paper collage. To get paper to the shape you require, you will need to tear or cut it. There are many ways that you can accomplish this first step of collage-making.

Tearing

It is very simple to pick up a piece of paper and tear a shape out of it. A torn edge can look very pleasing on its own or when placed next to a cut edge. Torn paper can often look surprisingly effective, once you've placed it in position.

Cutting

The main tools for cutting are scissors and craft knives. Used skilfully, they can both produce a variety of curved and straight lines.

A craft knife can cut shapes in paper as easily as a pencil can draw them. But a craft knife is sharp so always cut away from your body. Make sure the safety cover is replaced after use.

A cutting surface

If you're using a craft knife, you will need something to cut on. Card will do, but it must be thick. Rubber cutting mats are quite expensive, but will never wear out.

◀ The blue figure is torn from paper that is coloured on both sides. Some edges will be a lighter shade and have a different texture.

The pink figure is torn from paper that is coloured on one side only. If you tear a piece in half one of the strips will have a coloured edge, and one will be edged with a white line. This can look effective against a background of a different colour.

▲ A hole puncher can be used to create interesting effects. Here, holes in blue paper create the effect of falling snow.

▼ Special scissors called pinking shears create a regular V-shaped edge, which can look like grass.

▲ A craft knife makes clean lines. It is also good for cutting holes in the middle of paper, like the castle windows above.

▶ Folding or curling can make flat paper three-dimensional. The steps above were folded and the bird's plume was curled round a pencil. A torn straight edge can be created by tearing paper against a ruler. Scissors or a craft knife can be used to fringe paper.

Special Effects with Paper

Paper is a very flexible material which can be used in all sorts of different ways. Some of the special effects you can achieve are described here; you may also think of some new ones.

Changing texture

Paper usually has an even, uniform surface. But this texture or feel can be changed. Thin paper, such as tissue paper, can be crumpled and then flattened out again. Paper can also be pressed onto rough or textured surfaces and rubbed with a hard object like the back of a spoon to give it a different feel.

With tin foil you can create the impression of an object by wrapping foil around it and then lifting it off. The spoon below is an example.

▼ *"The collage below uses a number of techniques to produce a picture of the objects found on a kitchen table. I have crumpled purple tissue paper to imitate the skin of the prunes. To simulate the pitted surface of strawberries I pressed red paper over a sieve and rubbed it with a spoon."*

Fixing Paper Down

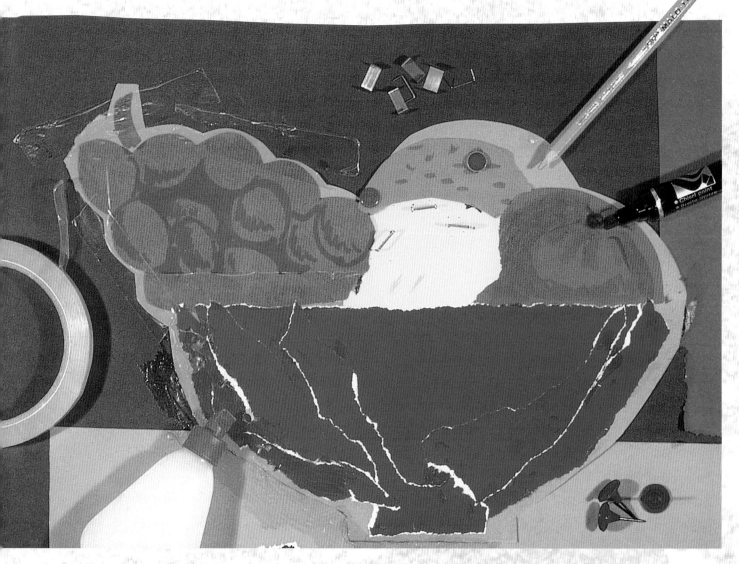

Drawing and painting

Try drawing or painting parts of paper to create a range of different effects. Coloured pencils, crayons, chalks, felt-tip pens and paints can all be used for this.

Gluing paper down

Once your paper is torn or cut and painted, you will need to attach it to the background of your collage. Gluing is the basic method. Most glues dry to a clear surface. Any glue left showing can be rubbed away.

▲ *"Above is a fruit bowl collage made with a combination of cut and torn shapes, painted and stuck down in a variety of ways. I used drawing pins and staples in the picture to look like pips and stalks of fruit."*

Sticky tape, pins and staples

Sticky tape can be used to fix paper down. Use double-sided tape on the back if you don't want it to show. You can use pins and staples to attach heavier papers to card, polystyrene or cork.

The World of Paper

Paper is an important resource for the collage artist. From tissue paper to newsprint, from postcards to writing paper, it's important to get to know the range of papers that are available.

A library of paper

For this project you will need lots of types of paper.

The aim is to find out what paper can do by putting together your own collage of petal shapes from different papers. Use as many textures as you can find.

Practising composition

If you pick a bunch of flowers, you will probably want to arrange them in a vase. In the same way, your paper flowers need to be arranged in a pleasing way. This is called composition. An advantage of collage is the ability to practise composition before deciding on and sticking down a final version.

▶ *"I have overlayed some flowers on the right. Using similar shapes will bring out the different qualities and textures of the paper."*

All about paper

The word 'paper' comes from the name of the papyrus plant that used to grow wild along the River Nile in Egypt about 4,000 years ago. Ancient Egyptians used to pound the leaves flat and use them to write on.

Today, almost all of the paper you use is made up of wood fibres. Wood fibres consist of tiny cellulose strands stuck together with a natural adhesive material called lignin. It's by separating and re-organizing these fibres that paper is made. Shown here are (1) corrugated paper, (2) notepaper, (3) tracing paper, (4) recycled paper and (5) wrapping paper.

Step by Step

Gathering your ingredients

Collage can involve a wide range of materials. This project is about working with more varied ingredients, and building a picture with them step by step.

Begin by assembling your raw materials. You might collect ready-made images, like postcards and photographs from magazines. You could also include different types of paper.

▼ 1. A mixture of torn and cut edges will add interest to your picture. Your paper shapes can be overlapped. Keep an open mind about where and at what angle the pieces might go.

▼ 2. Magazine images add colour and texture to your work. Remember that you can make alterations to your pictures before, and even after, sticking them down.

◄ *"Here are some of the materials I used for the jungle collage. I added some interesting odds and ends - bits of packaging material and other scraps of junk that would otherwise have been thrown away."*

Finding a subject

You may have an idea for your collage before you start, or an idea may come to you as you gather materials. To begin your collage, cut and tear simple shapes for some of the main themes in your collage (1).

Size and scale

Postcards and photographs (2) provide images for you to experiment with scale. Objects that are close to us look large, and those that are further away look smaller. Look at the images of animals on the left. The largest, the lion, belongs in the front of the picture. The medium-sized gorilla looks right in the middle, and the tiny bird looks best at the top, where it appears to be in the distance.

Putting it all together

It's time to see how your ingredients fit together (3). The junk can be brought into the picture to give it a three-dimensional look and a touch of humour. The elements of your collage are like a puzzle, but there is no right or wrong way to put them together. See what looks best to you.

▼ 3. Below is a finished collage. A milk bottle top has become the sun, and a piece of string has turned into a snake sunning itself on a rock. Strong glue was needed to fix these down securely.

Working with Colour

One of the joys of collage is being able to work with large areas of colour, without first having to mix paint, or to crayon laboriously. There's no better way to find out how colours work together.

Colours have many jobs to do

Colours express feeling and create mood and atmosphere. Colours can blend together or stand out. Colours can appear to change depending on which other colours they are placed next to. Warm colours such as yellows and reds seem to jump out, whereas cool colours such as blues and purples are more retiring. By positioning colours correctly, you can create a real sense of depth in your work.

Creating depth with colour

This project works best with tissue paper as it allows colours to show through one another.

To build up a land or a seascape, begin by laying down broad areas of colour. Use warm colours in the foreground, and cooler colours in the background. Overlapping colours creates subtle shades, like the turquoise at the water's edge in the collage shown.

▶ *"To get the tissue paper to lie flat, I put small spots of glue on either end of the torn strips and smoothed them down. When the background was finished, I added the details of the sun, boat and the bathers, to focus the eye on the different areas of the picture."*

▼ Warm colours advance towards you. They are right for the foreground of your picture. Cool colours recede; they fit best in the background of the picture.

▼ The eye is drawn to contrasting, or complementary, colours such as yellow and purple. Other contrasting pairs are red and green, and blue and orange.

▼ A single layer of transparent yellow or red paper laid over a white background looks pale and muted; a double layer looks darker and brighter. Overlapping different colours creates new ones. Here red and yellow are overlapped to make orange.

Exploring Tone

What is tone? Tone is about how light or dark something is. Tone gives shape to objects by showing where light falls on them. This project is about practising seeing tone by making a collage from newspaper.

Tone and lighting

Arrange some objects into a still life such as bottles and a glass on a table. The two factors that affect the tones are the colours of your objects – how light or dark they are – and the effect of light on them. For example, a pale highlight on a black jug could look lighter than a shadow on a white plate.

Matching tone

Study the effect of light on your arrangement and identify areas of tone in it. Look closely at the bottles and the glass on the table. Match what you see with the black, grey and white tones of your newspaper. Cut or tear shapes from paper of the right tone, and build up your picture.

▶ *"From the large black letters of the headlines to widely spaced lettering and small print, a newspaper contains all the tones you need for your still life. To make the job simpler, I put the background in first, and the paler shapes over it."*

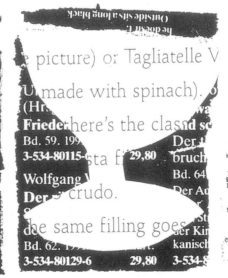

▲ A light shining from the side creates areas of pale tone and shadow on an object. Sometimes these are very distinct.

▲ If you place light and dark tones next to one another, it produces a dramatic effect. The eye is drawn to these areas.

▲ Cut shapes often convey abrupt changes in tone. A torn line can suggest one area of tone blurring into another.

▲ All colours have tones. If you look at the squares here, you may be able to identify particular colours, and the differences between their tones. Compare them to the tones on the newspaper. The more you look, the more tones you will see in the newspaper.

Marbling and Rubbing

Marbling paper is fun, and can produce amazing results for you to use in collage. You will need oil paint, linseed oil, turpentine, a bowl, some jam jars and a cover for your working surface.

Rubbings

Rubbings are impressions of textures. Look for objects with interesting textures. Place a sheet of thin paper over one, and rub the paper with coloured crayon, pencil, or chalk.

Marbling

Follow the steps below and you can make some interesting patterns.

▶ Use your rubbings and marbled papers to make a collage, perhaps a landscape, like the one on the right.

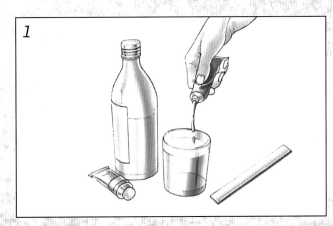

▲ In a jam jar, mix up one teaspoonful of linseed oil with two of turpentine. Add 15 centimetres of paint from a tube, and stir the mixture with a stick.

▲ Make up several jam jars with different colours. Fill a bowl with water. Pour in a jar of paint. The mixture will float on the water. Stir it again.

▲ Take a piece of plain paper and lay it on the surface of the water. Lift it off again almost immediately, and drain off the excess water. Lie it flat to dry.

▲ Your paper will now be marbled. You can immerse it again in another colour, or add a new colour to the water and try again with a fresh sheet.

Making a good impression

Below are some examples of different textures made by rubbing. Try making rubbings of coins and the grain of wood.

Many kitchen utensils also have interesting textures – try a cheese grater, a sieve and a straw table mat.

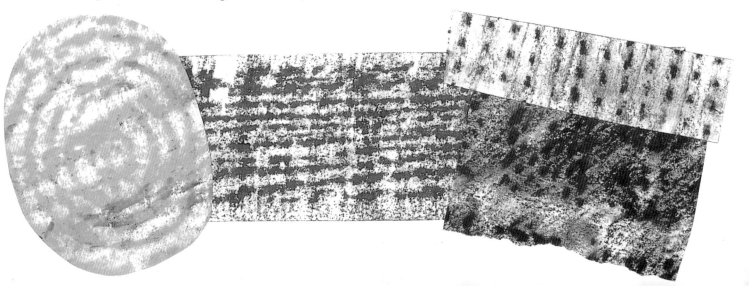

Working with Photos

"From this day on, painting is dead." Many people believed this when photography was invented. Artists today haven't given up painting, but a great many use photographs in picture-making.

Picture puzzles

Cutting up and reassembling pictures will produce new images which can be intriguing and funny. You will need a collection of images cut from photographs or magazines. Cut the images into squares, strips, or a shape like a fan. A fan shape can emphasise curves, such as a goose's neck.

Two into one *will* go

The project at the bottom of the opposite page works best with two images which complement each other. Cut both pictures into strips, combine the two images and the shapes will interact with one another.

▲ The image above is composed of squares. To cut squares more accurately, mark out the lines on the back of your image first.

The illustration shows any one of the many ways in which the squares can be reassembled. Try rotating each square by 90° and see what happens. Try again, rotating all the squares by 180° and sticking them down.

▲ Here, the photograph from the opposite page has been treated very differently. Try replacing strips like these in reverse order, or removing every other one and putting the rest together again.

▼ The curves of the hills echo the shape of the bird's head below. Look for similar shapes for your own collage.

Photomontage

A collage made up of a number of photographs is called a photomontage. Photomontages can often look more like pictures of dreams than of everyday life. Shapes can be repeated, and familiar images can be transformed into strange and bizarre ones. This project is about exploring the patterns you can make with repeated shapes. You will need a craft knife and photographs or magazines.

Repeating shapes

Look through your photographs and magazines and find an image that appeals to you. Choose a figure or a simple form that is easy to recognise from its outline or silhouette alone. Cut around the outline, pressing down hard on the magazine and cutting through several other pages as you do so. When you've cut out your outline, you will be left with a series of identical shapes (see the illustration below).

On the left below, the figure on the balcony (1) has been cut out and moved from its original setting (2), leaving the negative shape.

On the right, both figures and backgrounds have been turned over, to produce a series of shapes which mirror those on the left.

Positive and negative

You will also have a number of holes in the backgrounds, or 'negative shapes', as well as the positive ones of the figure itself. The idea is to work with these negative shapes as well as the positive ones in your collage and see what kind of image you can create.

Magazines are printed on both sides of the paper, so your positive and negative images will have parts of other pictures printed on the back of them. Collect a series of images

▲ *"I have put single leaves together in a group to transform them into whole trees. A cat's face has become a butterfly; its shape echoes the floating features of the face on the opposite side."*

and backgrounds. The montage above is based on the mirroring technique, and also on the dream-like transformation of one thing into another. Turn some over and see how they mirror the others.

21

Drawing with Collage

Your collage projects so far have involved the assembly and cutting of papers and objects to make a variety of compositions. In this project, a drawing or painting is supplemented by collage techniques.

Using collage fragments

Choose a subject for your drawing. This subject could be a street scene or the view from your window. See how you can add to your drawing. Newspaper headlines, patches of newsprint and magazine adverts can all enhance your drawing. Don't take the words on your fragments too literally – they don't need to match exactly with your drawing to fit in.

Mixing materials

The picture opposite was drawn in pencil, charcoal, brown oil pastel, and pen and ink. Leave spaces in your drawing for your collage fragments. Try out different compositions with your newspaper pieces. When you finish, glue them in place to make your picture.

▶ If your subject is a street scene, printed words and pictures can add a touch of realism to shop fronts, signs or billboards. If you find drawing people difficult, why not make them with collage instead?

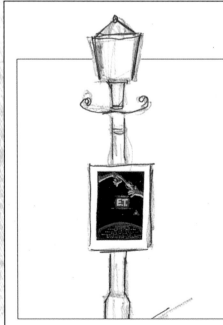

▲ To avoid smudging, spray your drawing with fixative before you glue in your chosen fragments.

▲ Alternatively, stick down your collage paper first. You can draw an image around it, without smudging.

▲ If you can't find a word, cut out separate letters and paste them down to spell the word out.

Working with Fabric

You don't have to be able to sew or knit to enjoy the rich world of cloth. Fabrics open up an entirely new range of possibilities, enabling you to achieve effects you can't get any other way.

Many textures

Collect as many different kinds of fabric as you can find. Silk, corduroy, velvet, hessian, muslin, wool and felt – each material has its own weave, texture and pattern. Buttons, sequins and lace can be added. You will need a pair of sharp scissors, strong glue, pins or staples, and thick cardboard or cork to use as a base for your collage.

What do your scraps suggest?

Study your pieces and see what they remind you of. You could try a head like the one here, a landscape, or an abstract pattern. Try your pieces in different positions before sticking or stapling them down.

▼ *"The odds and ends I collected suggested the crazy face and clothes of a clown. I chose white nylon for the face and a background of cotton drill, and began by laying down these basic ingredients.*

I chose shiny red cotton for the clown's nose, and small cotton patchwork squares for his jacket. I tried strands of wool for the hair, but finally opted for a coarse tweed material."

Three-dimensional Collage

Throughout this book, in gluing one piece of paper over another, you have been creating an image which is three-dimensional. This project is about developing this quality fully, and creating an image which really stands out!

A load of old rubbish

You will need to make a new collection, this time of junk! Old boxes, tubes, plastic bottles, toys, wood and leaves can all be used. You will need a base of wood, cork or polystyrene. Nails, staples or glue will fix the objects. Choose a subject – it could be a science fiction city scene with stairways and towers as shown here.

Using shadows

One of the advantages of 3-D collage is that the shadows cast by objects can become part of the design. When it's all fixed down, a coat of paint will unify your collage, and emphasise the play of light and shadow on it.

▶ Nails, pine cones, bark and the imprint of a car in foil have all been used on the right. The toys add a bit of extra interest.

Adapting your materials

Some of your ingredients will need to be transformed before they can be used. Open out some boxes, halve tubes and splay out plastic cups. Fold card to make steps and doors. Hide things inside others.

26

A Diary in Collage

It's said that every picture tells a story. Have you ever kept a scrapbook of a holiday you went on to remind you of the trip? This page is about using the bits and pieces connected with such a journey to make a three-dimensional collage.

Scrapbook journalism

If you have an old scrapbook, you have an opportunity to recycle all your old holiday souvenirs. If not, you will need to go on a special expedition to gather your materials. Try a trip to a gallery or a walk in the park to provide you with inspiration.

On your expedition

Plan a journey where you will find the materials that you need. Collect anything that might be effective in a collage, including tickets, maps, leaflets and postcards. Take snapshots, or draw sketches. You could decide to stop regularly, every hundred paces for example, and draw or pick up anything that looks interesting. The things you collect could be paper, balloons, coins, film and sand.

Composing your materials

When you get home, arrange your materials on a large sheet of card, or on a firm base. Test out your objects in different positions. You may decide to make a composition using objects in the order in which they were collected. Or you may compose something that simply makes the best arrangement. When you find the most pleasing composition, fix down your materials. Many modern artists have presented records of their journeys in this way.

◄ *"My collage records a trip to Disneyworld, but as you can see, the work is still in progress. Most of the materials have been positioned, but the objects bottom right have still to become part of the picture."*

Your own collage might include some of the ingredients below – brochures and postcards, maps, tickets and passes. You could also use 'found objects' such as twigs, leaves, flowers, earth and shells.

Gifts and Presentation

Collage offers a great way to produce many kinds of images, in quantity. These images can make excellent cards and posters.

Repeating yourself

By pressing hard through several layers of paper with a craft knife, or by cutting them with scissors, you can create a series of identical shapes. These shapes can be used to mass-produce cards or posters. On the left are identical posters for a school play, which were made in this way.

Varying composition

Identical shapes don't have to be arranged in the same way every time. On the right two party invitations are made with identical images but have different compositions. The shapes have been positioned at opposite angles, and even stuck in upside down. Glue your paper shapes onto stiff card for better results.

Presentation

Your collages will look even better when well presented. Some will look good with trimmed edges, mounted on card or framed behind glass. If your collage is made of freely torn shapes, the rough edges may look best untrimmed, mounted with a border of card showing on all sides.

Index

THE CURSE OF APOLLO'S GOLD

It seemed as if nothing could stop the Celtic warriors. They had taken Macedonia, once the home of Alexander, greatest general of the ancient world. They celebrated their victory with looted flagons of the local wine, which warmed their hearts and loosened their tongues. But their leader, Brennus, was more thoughtful than his men, and went off by himself to think:

'Why stop here? Just over those mountains is Greece, and beyond Greece, all the riches of the East. Alexander the Great went there – why shouldn't we?'

But Brennus had to persuade his men to follow him. He would be asking a lot, and must promise a lot in return. He could tell them about the riches of the Greek cities; but would that be enough? He decided to try a trick. From the Greek captives he had taken, he chose the shortest and weakest to parade in front of his troops. 'There!' he said, 'You can easily beat the Greeks – why, they're practically dwarfs!'

Soon Brennus had a huge army ready to invade Greece. But almost at once he met an obstacle. The Greeks had pulled down all the bridges over a great river in their path. Even the shallowest reaches were too deep to cross except on horseback. But dreams of treasure inspired Brennus's footsoldiers to find ways across. Some swam the river; others lashed their wooden shields together to make rafts.

Once across the river, Brennus planned to take Delphi – the greatest temple of Greece. It contained enormous amounts of gold, given to honour the god Apollo.

But between the Celts and the temple was a range of mountains, and the Greeks were guarding all the passes. Soon Brennus's men started to complain; they were an ill-disciplined army, and only the promise of treasure held them together. Brennus was desperate to find a way across the mountains before they all deserted him. He decided to distract the Greeks.

Brennus sent some soldiers out to devastate the neighbouring countryside. Many of the Greeks guarding the passes saw their homes being destroyed – and at once left to save them. In the morning mists, Brennus led his main force up the mountain. By the time the depleted Greek forces realised what was happening it was too late. The Celts fell savagely on the remaining guards, and soon the road to Delphi was clear.

However, the people of Delphi resisted harder than Brennus had expected. The battle for the temple was long and bloody. At last the Celts broke through the defenders and entered the temple. Some took the treasure away, but as they left the god took his revenge.

The earth shook under the raiders' feet, and great fissures opened in the ground, swallowing many of them up. Thunder drowned the Celts' cries of terror; a thick white blizzard of snow blinded them, and huge stones rained down from the sky. Apollo's temple was not to be easily violated!

The earth cracked open and swallowed up the invaders.

Practical Tips

Storing your materials

Many of the projects in this book have involved collecting materials and you will need to organise some storage space. Sort different kinds of paper into separate piles, and store them tidily.

Preparation

Collage can be untidy and messy work, so you will need to organise your working area. You will need a lot of space. Cover your surface with old cloths and wear old clothes. Keep tissues at hand to mop up spills. Replace the cap on your tube of glue, and cover your craft knife.

Gluing large areas

If you need to glue large areas of paper, wallpaper paste is ideal. The paste should be mixed with water in a jar.

Warning

The fumes of some kinds of glue are harmful. Be very careful not to breathe them in.

More tearing techniques

You can get a neat tear by lightly scoring a line in your paper first with a craft knife. Tear along the scored line for a slightly ragged edge, or press out the shape instead. Alternatively, draw the line you want with a paintbrush dipped in water, and then tear along it while the paper is still wet.

At a distance

Collages are pictures too, and they need the chance to be seen in their own right. Hang your work on a wall where it can be seen from a distance. Over a period of time, you may notice things you want to change. One of the great advantages of collage is that additions and alterations are almost always possible.

05